Cambridge **Discovery Education**™
▶ **INTERACTIVE READERS**

Series editor: Bob Hastings

THE SCIENCE OF HEAT

A2

Nic Harris

CAMBRIDGE
UNIVERSITY PRESS

DISCOVERY
EDUCATION™

CAMBRIDGE UNIVERSITY PRESS
Cambridge, New York, Melbourne, Madrid, Cape Town,
Singapore, São Paulo, Delhi, Mexico City

Cambridge University Press
32 Avenue of the Americas, New York, NY 10013-2473, USA

www.cambridge.org
Information on this title: www.cambridge.org/9781107697720

First published 2014

Printed in Hong Kong, China, by Golden Cup Printing Company Limited

A catalog record for this publication is available from the British Library.

Library of Congress Cataloging-in-Publication Data

Harris, Nicholas, 1956-
  The science of heat / Nic Harris.
      pages cm. -- (Cambridge discovery interactive readers)
  ISBN 978-1-107-69772-0 (pbk. : alk. paper)
  1. Heat--Juvenile literature. 2. English language--Textbooks for foreign speakers. 3. Readers
(Elementary) I. Title.

QC256.H37 2013
536--dc23

                                      2013016885

ISBN 978-1-107-69772-0

Additional resources for this publication at www.cambridge.org

Layout services, art direction, book design, and photo research: Q2ABillSMITH GROUP
Editorial services: Hyphen S.A.
Audio production: CityVox, New York
Video production: Q2ABillSMITH GROUP

Contents

Before You Read:
Get Ready!

What do you think about when you hear the word "hot"? Maybe a sunny day at the beach or a hot day in the office. It could be a hot drink or a hot shower. And what about colors? Is red hotter than blue? In this book we are going to look at hot places, hot things, and people in hot places all over the world.

Words to Know

Complete the sentences with the correct words.

sweat	desert	volcano
scientist	heat	blood

1 Your heart sends _____ to all parts of your body.

2 A _____ is often a very hot, dry place.

3 You use _____ when you cook food.

4 A _____ is a kind of mountain. Fire can come out of it.

5 When people run a lot, they _____ , and their faces become wet.

6 My father works as a _____ .

Words to Know

Read the paragraph. Then complete the sentences with the correct highlighted words.

The temperature in the Sahara Desert is very hot. Animals have to adapt to this hot and dry climate. They can do this in many ways. For example, some animals sleep in the day, when the temperatures are the hottest. People who live in deserts need to find ways to keep cool and to grow food. Many use something called irrigation to bring water from a river to their fields. Some desert people live near an oasis. This gives them water to drink and to use in their fields.

1 The _____ of Central America is rainy and warm all year, but in North Africa it's sunny and dry most of the time.

2 Summer days in my city are warm, but the nights are often _____ .

3 When you move to a new country, you must change and _____ to a new way of life.

4 Many farms use _____ to help grow plants.

5 An _____ is a pool of water in the middle of a very dry place.

CHAPTER 1

It's Too Hot!

PUT ON SOME SHORTS AND A T-SHIRT. TURN ON THE AIR CONDITIONING.[1] THIS BOOK IS GOING TO MAKE YOU FEEL HOT!

"Good morning everyone, you are listening to XYZ radio. And now the weather. It's going to be a very hot day today, with temperatures of 38° Celsius. Lots of sun and no clouds."

Are you happy when you hear this because you love the heat? Or are you unhappy because you hate the heat?

The dictionary says that "hot" means having a high temperature. But what does that tell us? Two people are sitting in a room together. One of them is sweating and wants to open the windows. The other is happily reading a book and loves the temperature. Different people feel comfortable at different temperatures. But why?

[1] **air conditioning:** makes the air inside buildings and cars cold

Well, sometimes your body can make a difference. People who are heavy usually don't like the heat as much as people who are thin.

A person's age is also important. Older people usually have more problems when it is hot. They don't sweat as easily or as much as young people. Do men's bodies adapt to the heat better than women's? Yes, men sweat more than women, so they are better at keeping their body temperatures normal when it is hot.

?

ANALYZE

Think about the last time you felt very hot. Where was it? What were you doing? Were you happy?

CHAPTER 2

Hot Places

MANY PLACES IN THE WORLD ARE SO HOT AND DRY IT IS NEARLY IMPOSSIBLE FOR PEOPLE TO LIVE THERE.

Deserts

The biggest and perhaps the most famous desert in the world is the Sahara, in Africa. It is about as big as the USA! If you look at a picture of this desert, you might think you are looking at a very big beach. In places like the Sahara, and other hot deserts, there are a lot of sand dunes (some as high as 180 meters) and rocks. There isn't much water in deserts because it doesn't rain much. When it does rain, it often rains very hard, but only for a short time. Because of the hot, dry air, the water quickly evaporates.[2]

[2]**evaporate:** when a liquid becomes dry from the heat and goes away

Sand dunes in the Sahara Desert

The Sahara is the biggest desert in the world, but is it the hottest? Not everyone agrees which is the hottest place in the world. It is difficult to say. Do we mean the highest ever temperature in one day? Or the highest temperature during a year? Or over many years? Let's look at some of the world's hot places. One day in 2008, the Turpan Basin in China had a temperature of 66.8°C in the shade![3] In 2003, the shade temperature in a part of Queensland, Australia, was 69.3°C. Think about living in the Lut Desert of Iran. A **thermometer** there showed a shade temperature of 70.7°C in 2005. Nobody could live very long in that temperature!

Volcanoes

If you think the Lut Desert is hot, what about deep inside the Earth? Scientists say the temperature there is about 7,000°C! This is so hot that the rock is not hard, it is a **boiling liquid** called magma.

[3] **shade:** somewhere that doesn't get the light from the sun

Most deserts are near the **equator.**

Volcanoes are mountains that have a lot of magma below them. There are about 1,500 volcanoes in different countries around the world and there are many more under the sea. Sometimes, the magma below a volcano becomes even hotter and moves towards the top. Suddenly, the top of the volcano breaks open, and thousands of kilograms of boiling magma and ash[4] fly up into the air. This is called a volcanic eruption.

Eruptions can be very dangerous. In 1883, a volcano on the island of Krakatoa, in Indonesia, erupted. Almost all of the island fell into the sea and 40,000 people lost their lives. People heard the sound of the eruption thousands of kilometers away.

[4]**ash:** when some things are put in fire, they become ash

A volcanic eruption

Mount Vesuvius, in Italy, has erupted many times in the past, most famously in 79 CE when it destroyed[5] the city of Pompeii. In 2011, an underwater volcano erupted near Japan. A tsunami[6] followed minutes after this and killed thousands of people.

So it's really hot deep inside the Earth, but it's much hotter in another place. When you are sitting on a beach and the temperature is 38°C, do you sometimes think about how hot it is on the Sun?

The heat from the Sun travels 150 million kilometers to get to you. In the center of the Sun, it is an amazing 15,000,000°C. Now that is hot!

[5]**destroy:** break something so it can't be used again
[6]**tsunami:** a very large and dangerous ocean wall of water that is made by an earthquake under the sea

Video Quest

Super Volcanoes

Watch this video to learn about the volcanoes of Yellowstone National Park. When did some very big eruptions happen in the USA? What did they change?

CHAPTER 3

How to Survive in the Heat

HEAT IS DANGEROUS, AND VERY HIGH TEMPERATURES CAN KILL. SOMETIMES IT'S REALLY IMPORTANT TO KEEP COOL.

A healthy person's body temperature is about 37°C. When people exercise, their body temperatures go up, and when they sleep, their body temperatures go down. This is normal. People feel comfortable when the temperature outside their bodies is between 20 and 27°C. However, if the outside temperature goes higher than 30°C, some people start to have problems. They may feel uncomfortable and tired.

If the temperature goes even higher, people can have serious[7] health problems. The most serious is called heatstroke. This happens when a person's body temperature is higher than 41° C. People with body temperatures higher than 40° C must see a doctor as soon as possible. If they don't, they could become very sick and even die.

Some people work in very hot places. Think of people working in restaurant kitchens or builders working outside in the heat of the sun. People with these kinds of jobs may have a lot of heat **stress** in their lives.

And some people live in places that are hot almost all the time. They have to learn how to adapt to too much heat and not enough water. For example, the Bushmen of the Kalahari and the Bedouin of the Middle East do not live in one place all the time. These tribes[8] move around looking for water, and they know where to find it. They carry their houses with them.

[7]**serious:** something that is very bad, dangerous
[8]**tribe:** a group of people who live together in one big family

The Bedouin wear special clothes that help to keep them cool. They wear long coats that **cover** all their body. The coats are thin, but they are made from wool. You might think this is unusual – people often wear wool to keep warm. But wool also keeps you cool because air can go through it. The Bedouin also wear a kind of hat that covers their head and part of their face. This means their heads do not get too hot from the sun.

Many desert people use irrigation to help them grow food. They take water that is under the **ground** or from rivers and put it on their fields.

What can you do when it's too hot? Think about a very hot summer day. The temperature is 38°C. How can you keep cool?

- Drink liquids! Water is the best. Natural fruit juice is also good.

- Eat small meals. Don't eat one big meal, because this makes your body hotter.

- Take showers. It's a good idea to have several showers during the day. But the showers shouldn't be too cold. About room temperature is best.

- Wear the right clothes. Your clothes should be light, and when you're outside, wear a hat.

And the last thing! Plan your day well so you don't have to hurry to do things. If you hurry, you have more stress and this makes you even hotter.

Video Quest

The Oasis at Siwa

Watch this video to learn about water at a desert oasis. How deep is the water under the Siwa Oasis? How many people live in Siwa?

Irrigation channels

CHAPTER 4

Animals of the Desert

A DESERT IS A VERY HARD PLACE FOR PEOPLE TO LIVE, BUT SOME ANIMALS LIVE THERE EASILY.

Animals have two different kinds of **blood**. Humans and animals like dogs and birds have warm blood. It doesn't matter if it is hot or cold outside, their body temperature stays the same most of the time. When a warm-blooded animal eats, it uses the food to heat its body. When it is hot, the animal sweats. The sweat evaporates, and this cools[9] the body down.

Other animals, snakes for example, are cold-blooded. They cannot keep their body temperatures the same most of the time. If it is hot outside, they are hot. If it is cold outside, they are cold.

You can find both cold-blooded and warm-blooded animals who call the desert their home.

....
[9]**cool:** make colder

Cold-blooded animals like to lie in the sun to heat up their blood. However, warm-blooded animals have a very different problem. They don't want their blood to get hotter. They need their blood temperature to always stay the same. So in hot places, they try to keep cool. If they don't, they could die.

A kind of desert cat, the bobcat, does not go out in the day. It looks for food at night when the temperatures are lower. Other animals, like desert rats and mice, build their homes under the ground. They do this because it is cooler there.

But perhaps the warm-blooded animal most adapted to life in the desert is the camel. For thousands of years, people have used the camel to travel across hot, dry deserts.

Camels are called "the ships of the desert."

Video Quest

Desert Camels

Watch this video to learn more about camels. How long can a camel live without water? How many liters of water can a camel drink in ten minutes?

CHAPTER 5

Hot Language

SOMETIMES WE USE THE WORD "HOT" TO TALK ABOUT MORE THAN THE WEATHER.

What do you think this means? "Simon is in very hot water with his parents." It is not nice to be in very hot water, so Simon must be feeling uncomfortable. In this example, "in hot water" means he did something bad, and his parents are angry with him.

And what does this mean? "The new Smartphone is selling like hotcakes." Hotcakes are good to eat, so a lot of people buy them. Here a lot of people are buying the Smartphone because they think it is very good.

ANALYZE

Think about the way "hot" is used here: "I can't believe this concert! Bon Iver are really hot tonight!" Is the group doing well or badly?

Some Smartphones sell like hotcakes.

And this? "The problem is a hot potato for the president." It hurts to hold a hot potato in your hands. You want to throw it away. So the president has a very big problem, and he would like it to go away.

And the last one: "Simon is a hothead." When people get angry, their head and face become red and hot. Simon often gets angry very quickly, so people say he is a hothead.

CHAPTER 6

What Do You Think?

SOMETHING WE HEAR A LOT ABOUT TODAY IS CLIMATE CHANGE. THE EARTH IS GETTING HOTTER, AND THIS IS HAPPENING VERY FAST.

Today, we have many more factories and cars than we did 100 years ago. These make a gas called carbon dioxide, or CO_2. This gas goes into the **atmosphere**, and it stops heat from leaving the Earth. Scientists call this the **greenhouse effect**.

A few scientists say that people are not making climate change happen. They say it is natural. It is true that the temperature of the Earth changed in the past, but most scientists believe that climate change today is happening because of the way people live.

?

EVALUATE

Think of people living in the future. How will their lives be different when the climate is much hotter and drier than today?

So why is climate change a problem? A very small change in the temperature of the Earth can be very bad. The ice in the Arctic and the Antarctic begins to **melt**. Animals that live on the ice, like polar bears, may die. When the ice melts, there is more water in the sea, and the sea gets higher. That's no problem if you live on a mountain. But if you live near the sea, your home or even your country could soon be under water.

Surprisingly, climate change can bring a few good things. In places like the Arctic, a warmer climate means that new kinds of plants and flowers can grow and different animals can also live there.

After You Read

Read the following sentences and choose Ⓐ, Ⓑ, or Ⓒ.

1 The Sahara Desert is the most famous because it _____.

  Ⓐ is the hottest
  Ⓑ is the largest
  Ⓒ has no rain

2 Mount Vesuvius in Italy _____.

  Ⓐ never erupted in the past
  Ⓑ erupted once in the past
  Ⓒ erupted many times in the past

3 When people are sleeping, their body temperature _____.

  Ⓐ stays the same
  Ⓑ gets hotter
  Ⓒ gets cooler

4 When it is hot, people should _____.

  Ⓐ not eat a lot of food
  Ⓑ eat a big breakfast
  Ⓒ eat a lot at night

5 Desert rats live under the ground because it is _____.

  Ⓐ safer there
  Ⓑ not as hot there
  Ⓒ drier there

6 If someone is in hot water, they _____.

  Ⓐ are feeling very good
  Ⓑ did something wrong
  Ⓒ are feeling sick

7 A hothead is someone who is _____.

  Ⓐ always happy
  Ⓑ very clever
  Ⓒ often angry

8 When ice on the Earth melts, _____ .

   (A) there is more rain

   (B) the seas get higher

   (C) the weather gets colder

Complete the Text

Use the words in the box to complete the text.

boiling   covered   desert   heat   snake   sweating

Hi John,

   I'm on holiday in Morocco. It's very beautiful here but the temperature is **1** _____ hot. Yesterday, I went on a trip into the **2** _____ . I saw a lot of sand dunes and rocks. I also saw a **3** _____ and I was very afraid. It is a very dangerous animal. I was **4** _____ all day and my T-shirt was very wet. I **5** _____ my head with a hat but the **6** _____ was too much. 40° C! I had to go back to the hotel early.

?

EVALUATE

There are things we can do to stop climate change from happening. How helpful are these actions? Give each action a number from 1 to 5 (1 = not helpful, 5 = very helpful).

a. Don't travel by car in the city. Use a bicycle. _____
b. Use the heat from the sun to heat the water in your house. _____
c. Turn off the TV, lights, and computers when you are not using them. _____
d. Put on more clothes when you are cold in the house. Don't turn on the heating. _____
e. Don't buy more food than you need. _____

Answer Key

Words to Know, page 4

1 blood **2** desert **3** heat **4** volcano **5** sweat **6** scientist

Words to Know, page 5

1 climate **2** cool **3** adapt **4** irrigation **5** oasis

Analyze, page 7

Answers will vary.

Video Quest, page 11

The eruptions happened about two million years ago. The eruptions changed the area around them, and they changed the life of the plants and animals. Ash covered most of Western America.

Video Quest, page 15

The water is three kilometers under the ground. 30,000 people live in Siwa.

Video Quest, page 17

A camel can live for more than a week without water. A camel can drink 100 liters of water in ten minutes.

Analyze, page 19

Bon Iver is doing well.

Evaluate, page 21

Answers will vary.

Choose the Correct Answers, page 22

1 B **2** C **3** C **4** A **5** B **6** B **7** C **8** B

Complete the Text, page 23

1 boiling **2** desert **3** snake **4** sweating **5** covered **6** heat

Evaluate, page 23

Answers will vary.